...nus

and Neptune

Rosalind Mist

QED

Editor: Lauren Taylor
Designer: Melissa Alaverdy
Educational consultants:
    Heather Adamson
    and Jillian Harker

Copyright © QED Publishing
2013

First published in
the UK by QED Publishing,
A Quarto Group Company
230 City Road
London EC1V 2TT

www.qed-publishing.co.uk

ISBN 978 1 78171 215 3

Printed in China

A catalogue record for this
book is available from the
British Library.

Picture credits
(fc=front cover, t=top, b=bottom,
l=left, r=right, c=centre)

NASA fc JPL 1t, Johns Hopkins
University Applied Physics
Laboratory/Southwest Research
Institute 1b, JPL 4-5, 13t, 15b
Science Photo Library David A.
Hardy, Futures: 50 years in space
2-3, Mark Garlick 5b, Roger
Harris 8-9, John Chumack 10-11,
Mark Garlick 13b, Detlev van
Ravenswaay 14b, Walter Meyers 16-
17, 17t, Friedrich Saurer 18b, Mark
Garlick 19c, Detlev van Ravenswaay
19b, David A. Hardy, Futures: 50
years in space 20-21, Chris Butler
22, Friedrich Saurer 23t,
Shutterstock Jetrel 2-3, jupeart
4-5, 6-7, Marcel Clemens 12-13,
Irina Solatges 12-13, Jetrel 14-15,
Michelangelus 18-19, Paul Prescott
19t, jupeart 22-23, Jetrel 23t,
Jacopin 23b, thrashem 24

Words in **bold** appear in the
Glossary on page 24.

Contents

Uranus

Uranus is the third largest **planet** in the **Solar System**. It is the seventh planet from the **Sun**. Uranus is made mostly of gas.

Uranus is strange because it spins on its side.

5

The Solar System

The Solar System is made up of the Sun and all the things that move around it. A force called **gravity** holds it together. We cannot see gravity.

Neptune

Uranus

Saturn

Jupiter

Mars

Earth

Mercury

Sun

Days and years

A year on Uranus is 84 Earth years. A year is the time it takes a planet to go around the Sun once.

A day on Uranus is about 17 hours. A day is the time a planet takes to spin once.

Discovery

For thousands of
years, people knew
there were five planets.

They could see them
moving slowly in the sky.

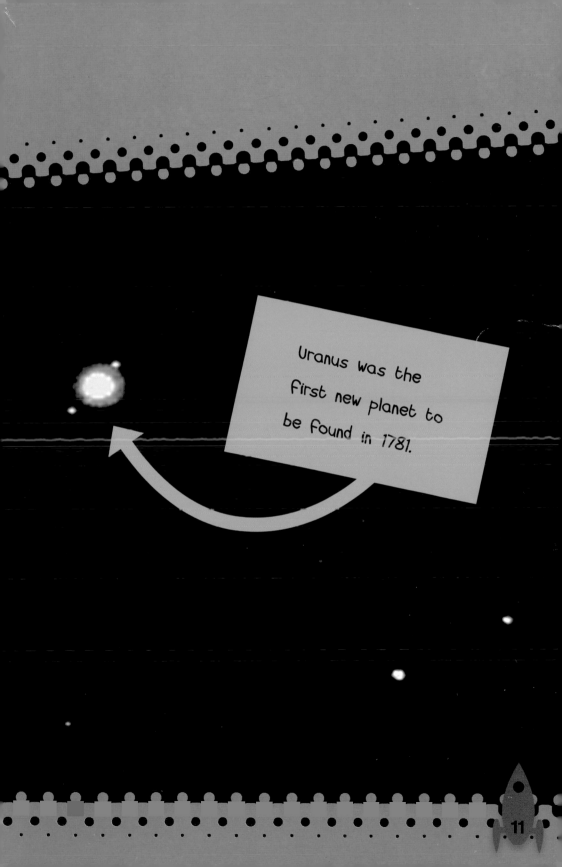

Uranus was the first new planet to be found in 1781.

Moons

Uranus has at least 27 moons. The five biggest moons are Miranda, Ariel, Umbriel, Titania and Oberon.

Umbriel

Miranda

Neptune

Uranus

Neptune has 13 moons.
Its biggest moon
is Triton.

Ariel

Titania

Oberon

13

Neptune

Neptune is the furthest planet. It is the fourth largest planet in the Solar System. Neptune is very far away.

Uranus

Sun

Neptune

Rings

Uranus and Neptune have rings. The rings of Uranus go from top to bottom. Neptune's rings go from side to side.

Neptune

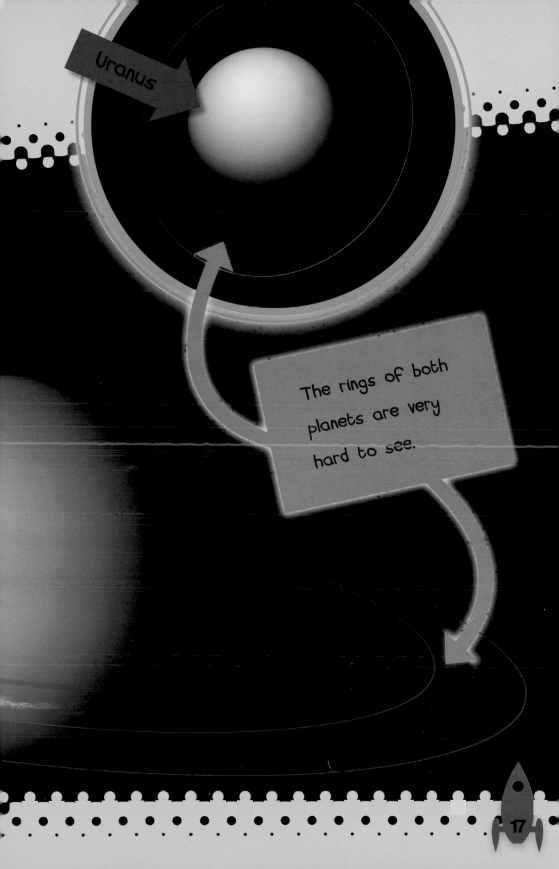

Dwarf planets

Dwarf planets are large objects that go around the Sun. They are not big enough to be true planets. So far we know of five dwarf planets. These are called Pluto, Eris, Ceres, Haumea and Makemake.

Eris

Haumea

Earth

Ceres

Pluto

Makemake

Pluto

Pluto is smaller than the Earth's Moon. It is even further away than Neptune. It is very cold with lots of ice.

Pluto

Sun

Pluto has three moons.
Charon is Pluto's biggest
moon. It is half the size
of Pluto!

Eris and Ceres

Eris is very far away. It is three times further than Pluto. Between Mars and Jupiter there is a band of rocks called **asteroids**. This is where Ceres can be found.

Ceres

Eris

asteroids

Glossary

asteroids – small rocky objects that move around the Sun

dwarf planet – a round object that moves around the Sun but is too small to be a planet

gravity – the force that pulls things towards each other

moon – a natural object that moves around a planet

planet – one of the eight large objects circling the Sun

rings – bands of dust and small rocky pieces that orbit some planets

solar system – the Sun and all of the things that move around it

Sun – the star that the Earth and the planets move around